Praise for the Fantastically Great Women books

"With their playful use of speech bubbles and perspective shifts, Pankhurst's books remain significantly more engaging and inspiring than the rival *Rebel Girls*."
Imogen Russell Williams, *The Guardian*

"It's a tremendously engaging read: smart, informative, inclusive and accessible, with gorgeous, visually creative art. The tone is really joyful and it's hard to imagine any group of primary-aged children who wouldn't be inspired by these stories."
Fiona Noble, *The Bookseller*

"So many worthy nonfiction books for this age group have good intentions but fail to step beyond simple preaching with boring line drawings. This one succeeds, thanks to its interesting choice of role models, gorgeous colourful illustrations, a sense of humour and sharp language that informs without patronising."
The Times

FANTASTICALLY GREAT WOMEN

SCIENTISTS and their STORIES

Books by
Kate Pankhurst

Fantastically Great Women
Who Saved the World

Fantastically Great Women
Who Made History

Fantastically Great Women
Who Worked Wonders

Fantastically Great Women
Who Saved the Planet

STUNNING!

Kate Pankhurst

FANTASTICALLY GREAT WOMEN

SCIENTISTS and their STORIES

BLOOMSBURY
CHILDREN'S BOOKS
LONDON OXFORD NEW YORK NEW DELHI SYDNEY

First published 2021 by Bloomsbury Publishing Plc
50 Bedford Square, London, WC1B 3DP
29 Earlsfort Terrace, Dublin 2, Ireland
www.bloomsbury.com

Bloomsbury is a registered trademark of
Bloomsbury Publishing Plc

978 1 5266 1533 6

Printed and bound by CPI Group (UK) Ltd, Croydon CRO 4YY

10 9 8 7 6 5 4 3

For Simon and Otto,
my fantastically great boys.

Contents

Women in Science

Women have been responsible for many of
the world's most groundbreaking scientific
discoveries and adventures. They've worked tirelessly
in laboratories, in the field, in the back of trucks
during the war and even in spaceships – all because
they wanted to find out more about the world we
live in, and beyond.

Yet, lots of female scientists' stories don't get told. Most people have heard of MARIE CURIE, who discovered two new **elements**, leading to a treatment for **cancer**, and won two Nobel Prizes. But they probably haven't heard of **Katia Krafft**, the fearless scientist who dedicated her whole life to studying **volcanoes** and even camped inside one! Or **TU YOUYOU**, the determined chemist who spent months on a remote island away from her family trying to invent a **medicine** for the life-threatening disease malaria – and succeeded.

Their achievements were extraordinary – so, why doesn't everyone know their names?

In the past, many people believed that science was a job for men. They didn't think that women could be **physicists** or **chemists**, **doctors** or **astronauts**, and they definitely didn't think women should be hanging around active volcanoes! They thought women just weren't as smart, and that it would be better if they stayed at home to look after their husbands and children.

Because of this, women were not always given the same education as men. Many schools and universities did not accept female students. And even when they did, some families still forbade their daughters from going. As a child, CAROLINE HERSCHEL, who was the first professional female astronomer, wasn't allowed to go to school because her parents wanted her to be a servant instead. Women also faced **prejudice** because of where they came from, how much money they had and the colour of their skin.

Many women fought against these stereotypes and proved them wrong. Botanist **Janaki Ammal** called off her arranged marriage – she wanted to do a **Master's degree** instead. Elizabeth Blackwell showed the world exactly why we need female doctors. And MAE JEMISON made history when she became the first African-American woman to soar into space.

HUMPH.

But it wasn't always easy. Even once women were allowed to study and work at universities, often they weren't given proper laboratories to work in, weren't paid the same as male scientists and weren't always given the credit for their work. It was **Rosalind Franklin** who first discovered the double helix structure of **DNA**, but most people think it was **James Watson** and **Francis Crick**.

This book tells the stories of just some of the most incredible female scientists the world has ever seen and the work they did. They lived at different times and came from many different countries and backgrounds. But they have a few things in common …

They were smart, inquisitive and persistent.

They NEVER GAVE UP on their DREAMS.

And, not only did they change the world's understanding of science, they transformed people's ideas of what women can do.

Prepare to be inspired!

THE ASTRONAUT WHO REACHED FOR THE STARS...
MAE JEMISON

When **MAE JEMISON** watched the first **SPACE MISSIONS** on TV as a little girl, she knew that she'd become an astronaut one day.

Mae was born in Alabama, USA, in **1956**, just as the **Civil Rights Movement** was taking off. Black Americans had been treated badly for many years, particularly in the southern states. There were strict laws that kept white and black people separate. Black people often had to go to different schools and weren't allowed to work in certain jobs. This was called **segregation**. But now people like **ROSA PARKS** and **MARTIN LUTHER KING** were demanding equal rights for everyone. There were protests, arguments and fighting.

5

When Mae was eight, the US government finally passed laws saying that all Americans should have **EQUAL RIGHTS** – this meant women and people of colour should be treated the same way as white men. Now they could vote and get the same jobs. But even though the law had changed, lots of people **DIDN'T CHANGE THEIR MINDS**, and still thought black people were inferior.

WE HAVE RIGHTS!

When we JUDGE PEOPLE by what their BODIES LOOK LIKE instead of what they do and who they are it is called PREJUDICE. RACISM and SEXISM are two kinds of PREJUDICE

Sometimes PREJUDICE is EASY to RECOGNISE, like LAWS that say BLACK PEOPLE can't mix with WHITE PEOPLE

Sometimes it isn't SO OBVIOUS like when people think it's NORMAL for WHITE MEN to be in CHARGE or ASSUME girls aren't INTERESTED in SCIENCE

Hardly anyone in the **1960s** imagined that a black woman could be a scientist. Mae's favourite TV programme, *Star Trek*, had a black female officer called Uhuru on board the Starship Enterprise, but that was science fiction. When **NASA** sent real astronauts into space, they were mainly all white men.

Uhura, READY FOR ACTION!

Some black women worked at NASA during the **Space Race**, like **KATHERINE JOHNSON**, **DOROTHY VAUGHAN** and **MARY JACKSON**, but it took years before they became famous for their amazing work.

Mae was cross that there weren't any female astronauts – and **VERY** cross that nobody could give her a good reason why not.

She spent ages in libraries, reading about **SCIENCE** and **astronomy**, and learning about black American scientists and doctors. She studied the world around her – not just the stars, but animals, flowers, plants and the human body. She was **curious** about all the amazing things our bodies do, even the things that some people thought were **DISGUSTING**.

Mae learned a lot of other **SKILLS** too.

She learned to **SEW** and to design clothes for her dolls and then for herself ...

Mae also loved to **DANCE**! She could do all kinds of dance, including ballet, jazz and African. She performed on stage!

Mae was a **brilliant student**. Aged **SIXTEEN**, she went to Stanford University, one of the top colleges in America, to study **ENGINEERING**. At the time, very few white or black women did engineering. Some of the teachers treated Mae worse than white men in the same class.

Mae didn't let unfair teachers put her off. She got her engineering degree and studied African and Afro-American history too.

Then she had to make a decision. She wanted to train as a doctor, but she still loved dancing. Should she be a doctor or a dancer? As always, her mother had some **brilliant advice**.

Mae went to medical school – but she kept taking dance classes.

"You can always DANCE if you are a doctor, but you can't DOCTOR if you are a dancer."

When Mae started to study surgery, she realised she could apply the **SKILLS** she'd learned from making clothes. Designing clothes had taught her how things are put together.

In fact, lots of the skills Mae had learned in childhood were **EXTREMELY USEFUL** in her job as a scientist. When she taught herself to bake, her understanding of chemistry helped her get the bread right!

BEEP...
BEEP...
beep...

Mae worked for a little while as a doctor, but she wanted to do more. She joined the **Peace Corps**, a US government programme that sends **VOLUNTEERS** to work with governments, charities and businesses. She spent a couple of years working as a doctor in Liberia and Sierra Leone, which are very poor countries in West Africa.

Just after Mae arrived in Sierra Leone, a volunteer fell ill. Mae quickly realised he had **MENINGITIS** with **DANGEROUS** complications. There were no local hospitals that could give him the treatment he needed, so she ordered him to be taken to Germany right away on a special plane. But there was a problem – the US Embassy staff didn't believe this young black woman had the **RIGHT** to order a very expensive emergency flight.

Hmm.

I NEED a plane. NOW!

I'll get you to HOSPITAL.

Mae was an **EXPERIENCED DOCTOR** by now. She told the Embassy staff the flight was vital, and she didn't need anyone's permission to order it! She got her plane and stayed awake looking after her patient for **fifty-six hours** until they reached the German hospital. **The patient survived.**

Mae loved being a doctor, but she'd never forgotten her dream of **REACHING THE STARS**. In **1983, SALLY RIDE** became the first American woman to go into space. Now, at last, it seemed possible. Mae applied to NASA's astronaut training programme. In **1987**, she was accepted. Mae was so excited! But she had to wait several years before she was sent on **A MISSION**. First, she had to have **ASTRONAUT TRAINING** ...

NASA
Dear Mae,
Prepare to
begin
astronaut
training.
x

ASTRONAUT

WELCOME TO ASTRONAUT SCHOOL. YOU WILL BE BUSY!

FIG 1: LEARN HOW THE SPACE SHUTTLE WORKS

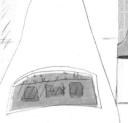

Practise using space technology inside this life-size model shuttle.

SO MUCH to learn!

FIG 2: EXPERIENCE THE EFFECTS OF ZERO GRAVITY

NASA have a special reduced-**gravity** aircraft that goes into free fall so passengers can experience **weightlessness**. This makes people sick so often that the plane is nicknamed the Vomit Comet!

VOM COM

SICK BAG

FIG 3: WALK LIKE AN ASTRONAUT

Astronauts practise space walks underwater in a huge swimming pool!

Walking UNDERWATER is like walking in ZERO gravity.

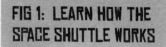

TRAINING

FIG 4: MASTER MOVING THINGS IN LOW GRAVITY

It's easy to start moving heavy things, but, because there is no friction, it's very hard to make them stop!

FIG 5: CALMLY DEAL WITH EMERGENCIES IN SPACE

FIG 6: KNOW WHAT TO DO IF A CREW MATE BECOMES SICK

Finally, in **1992**, Mae stepped on board the space shuttle Endeavour and prepared herself for a **BIG ADVENTURE** ...

THREE ...

TWO ...

ONE ....

NASA
Endeavour

BLAST OFF!

16

It's HAPPENING!

MAE JEMISON WAS THE FIRST BLACK WOMAN ASTRONAUT!

MISSION SPECIALIST

My space trip was a joint US and Japan mission called Spacelab-J, and I was a mission specialist. I launched **satellites** and went on space walks.

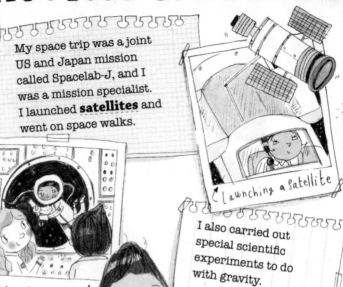

← Launching a satellite

SPACE WALKS ↑

I also carried out special scientific experiments to do with gravity.

On Earth we are weighed down by the force of GRAVITY all the time. But have you ever been in a roller coaster or a lift when it suddenly goes down and you feel like you are floating? That's the feeling of WEIGHTLESSNESS because you are in FREE FALL.

In space, weightlessness lasts all the time. There's no 'up' or 'down' when gravity isn't pulling you around! It is hard to get used to and can make astronauts feel tired, sick and dizzy.

MAE JEMISON'S LOG

If people spend too long in space, their muscles and bones **GET WEAKER** because they aren't using them enough. Many astronauts stay fit by exercising on gym machines like fixed bikes. But Mae also danced! **SHE LOVED DANCING IN SPACE.**

I feel FREE! I can do WONDERFUL lifts and spins and never come down!

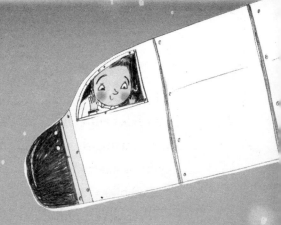

Up in the stars, Mae looked down at
Earth and thought how **BEAUTIFUL**
it was. Being in space gave her a
feeling of belonging to the **ENTIRE**
UNIVERSE. She decided she wanted
to do more to help people, and to
help the planet too ...

When Mae returned to Earth, lots of people asked her if she was happy to be the first black woman in space. She said, No! Mae thought other women should have had the chance too.

"I'm not the first Woman of colour, the first African American woman, who had the skills, the talent, the desire to be an astronaut. I happen to be the first one that NASA selected."

Mae had made history aged just **THIRTY-TWO**, but she wanted to change the world in other ways. She wanted everyone to have a chance to follow their dreams and use their talents. And she wanted to do more to save the Earth. Mae left NASA in **1993**, and set up a company to find ways science and technology can work with people's daily lives. She thought that we could solve more problems if **PEOPLE** work together. Science isn't just for inside the lab – it can **IMPROVE THE LIVES AND HEALTH** of people all over the world.

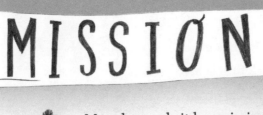

MISSION

Mae also made it her mission to encourage more **CHILDREN** to study science. She set up an **international science camp** for children, where students learn to think like a scientist and tackle **BIG QUESTIONS** about how we live, how science works in our daily lives and the future of the planet. The children also play sports, games, do cultural activities and **WATCH THE SKY AT NIGHT**, just like Mae did when she was little.

She's now working on a big project to get children interested in where food comes from.

The Milky Way

Mae has never been back into space. Instead, she is working on an international project to send people to a star outside of the **MILKY WAY**.

Who will go next? Will it be you?

When Mae was a little girl, a lot of people didn't think a black girl could grow up to be a doctor, a scientist and an astronaut. **MAE NEVER LISTENED TO THOSE PEOPLE.** She always said ...

"NEVER be limited by other people's limited imaginations!"

If other people can't imagine you doing something, then they need more imagination. Mae Jemison imagined herself reaching the stars – and that's exactly what she did.

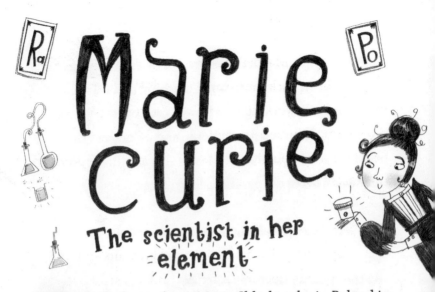

Marie Curie

The scientist in her element

Marie Curie was born Maria Skłodowska in Poland in **1867,** the youngest child of five. Her family called her Manya. Her parents worked hard as teachers, but it was difficult for them to make enough money to support their BIG family. When Manya was just ten years old, her mother became very sick and died. Her father had to bring up five young children all on his own.

THE SKŁODOWSKA FAMILY

Father

Mother

Józef

Manya

Bronya

Zofia

Helena

Although they had **little money**, Manya's father did the best for his children. He **loved** teaching and learning and wanted his children to have a **good education**, so he taught them science at home and often set Manya difficult maths problems. Manya was a brilliant student and was always desperate to learn more.

But learning more wasn't very easy.

At the time, Poland was ruled by Russia and there were **very strict** rules around education – what was taught and who was allowed to learn it. **Polish universities didn't accept women**.

SO CLEVER!

I LOVE learning.

For a while, Manya and her older sister Bronya attended the Flying University, an **illegal secret** group made up of young men and women who wanted to study traditional Polish scholarship, including the stuff the Russian government had forbidden. The classes met at night in different locations, so they wouldn't get caught. If they were they could be **arrested**. It was **dangerous**, but incredibly exciting.

Manya and Bronya wanted to study abroad in a proper university. But to do this was **expensive**. The sisters agreed that Manya would work as a governess to help pay for Bronya to **study medicine** in Paris, France. Once Bronya began to earn her own money, she would return the favour and help pay for Manya's education.

Manya became a governess to a rich factory-owner's children. But she didn't think it was **fair** that the rich children should learn while many of the peasant children from the village were not able to go to school. So, in her spare time, she decided to **teach them too**.

After three years, in **1891**, Manya's turn to study finally came and she went to the world-famous **Sorbonne University** in Paris. There, she took her Master's degree in physics and won a scholarship to do a maths degree too.

She changed her name to Marie **to try and fit in.**

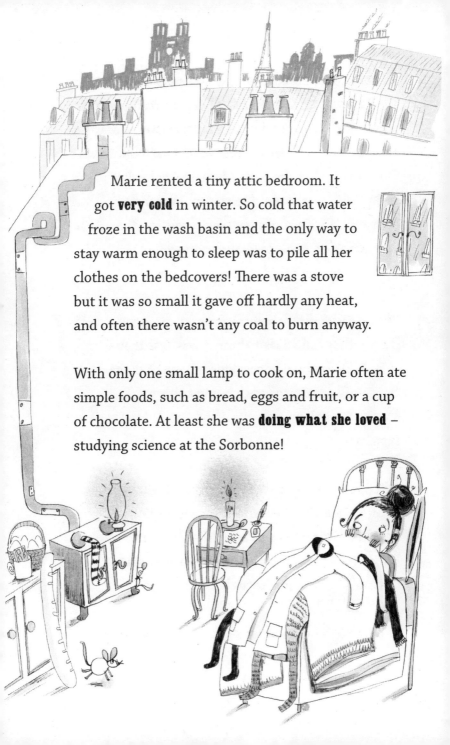

Marie rented a tiny attic bedroom. It got **very cold** in winter. So cold that water froze in the wash basin and the only way to stay warm enough to sleep was to pile all her clothes on the bedcovers! There was a stove but it was so small it gave off hardly any heat, and often there wasn't any coal to burn anyway.

With only one small lamp to cook on, Marie often ate simple foods, such as bread, eggs and fruit, or a cup of chocolate. At least she was **doing what she loved** – studying science at the Sorbonne!

After she graduated, Marie got a **research job** studying the **chemical structure of steel**, but to do the work she needed laboratory space. Luckily, one of Marie's friends put her in touch with **Pierre Curie**, who was the Lab Chief at the Paris Municipal School of Industrial Physics and Chemistry. When they met, Pierre could see how clever Marie was, so he immediately agreed to let her share the lab space.

Such CHEMISTRY!

They quickly became friends and, soon, they **fell in love**. Pierre asked Marie to marry him. Marie loved Pierre, but she wanted to go back home and work in Poland.

Marie refused his proposal and went home to visit her family and look for jobs. However, Polish universities still didn't accept female staff. Marie realised that there was **no future** for her in her homeland.

Marie returned to France and married Pierre in July **1895**. She bought a **dark blue outfit** instead of a frilly, white wedding dress, so she could **wear it in the lab**!

Hello baby Irène.

She had her first baby, **Irène**, in **1897**. Many women gave up their jobs when they had a baby, but Marie and Pierre **refused to consider that**. Pierre's father moved in to help take care of the baby, and Marie went back to work at the end of **1897**.

Pierre was now Professor of Physics at the Municipal School. Marie was given a converted shed next to the main building to work in. It was **cluttered** and **damp** and the roof leaked, but it was hers!

Marie wanted to do a **doctorate**. No woman had yet been awarded a doctorate in science anywhere in the world. Marie needed to choose an interesting subject to research – she knew **exactly** what that would be ...

An X-ray!

In **1895**, **Wilhelm Röntgen** had discovered a new kind of **ray**, which could pass through skin and muscle, allowing him to photograph the bones beneath. He called these mysterious rays **X-rays**.

The next year, **Henri Becquerel** discovered that the heavy metal **uranium** gave off a different kind of ray that could pass through metal.

Marie decided to research **Becquerel rays**.

X is often used to mean something unknown.

First, she checked Becquerel's observations about his rays. This is very important in science. It's not enough to discover something – other people must be able to do the **same experiment** and get the **same results**.

Becquerel had shown that uranium rays **electrically charge** the air they pass through. Marie measured this using a device that Pierre and his brother had invented, although the air in her leaky shed was so damp that it interfered with her measurements. She also confirmed that the amount of uranium rays **emitted** depended on the amount of uranium in a **compound**.

Then, Marie had an idea that would **change the**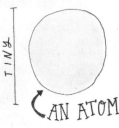
world – what if Becquerel rays weren't being
produced by chemical reactions, but
instead came from inside the uranium
atoms? If she was right, this would
mean that the accepted ideas about
atoms were **wrong**.

ATOMS

At the time, scientists believed matter
was made up of atoms – tiny particles.
The word 'atom' comes from an Ancient
Greek word meaning something that
can't be divided, because they thought an
atom was the smallest thing there was.

TINY

AN ATOM

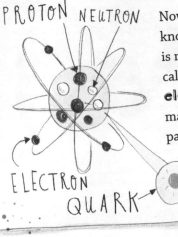

PROTON   NEUTRON

ELECTRON

QUARK

Now, after many years, we
know this is wrong. An atom
is made up of tinier particles
called **protons**, **neutrons** and
electrons, which are in turn
made up of incredibly tiny
particles called **quarks**.

Marie set out to discover if other elements or **minerals** would emit Becquerel rays. Pierre gave up his own research to work with her.

Marie discovered other compounds that emitted rays just like uranium did. She invented the word **radioactive** to describe them. She found that two uranium **ores**, **chalcocite** and **pitchblende**, emitted many more rays than pure uranium.

CHALCOCITE

PITCHBLENDE

After lots of hard work, Marie and Pierre

Did these MINERALS contain something even more RADIOACTIVE?

identified what they believed were two **unknown radioactive elements**.

Marie called the first one polonium, after Poland, and the second one radium. Polonium was **300** times more radioactive than uranium, and radium was **MILLIONS** of times more radioactive.

R a
RADIUM

P o
POLONIUM

Next, Marie had to isolate the **elements** and produce them in pure form. After three years, Marie isolated **one tenth of a gram** of pure radium chloride.

Radium had some odd effects. Its rays could make certain materials **glow** in the dark. It could be dangerous too – when Pierre attached a tube of radium to his arm for ten hours, the skin underneath was **damaged**. Radium rays could kill human cells! This was an incredible discovery for scientists looking for a **cure for cancer** – a disease where cells grow too quickly.

WARNING!
Radium is very harmful. Today, scientists are more careful when doing experiments and always wear protective gloves, clothing and goggles.

Newspapers talked about radium as if it was **magic** and a lot of people made money out of it – but Pierre and Marie never did. **They worked because they loved science, not to make money.**

37

By now **people all over the world** were talking about the **Curies**. They were invited to the **Royal Institution in Britain** to present their discoveries, but Marie was **not allowed** to lecture because she was a woman. Pierre gave the talk instead, but **he made sure everyone knew** that the research was Marie's idea.

My wife, Marie Curie, is a GENIUS.

ROYAL INSTITUTION

PIERRE CURIE

I don't feel so good.

Me either.

Pierre was also made **Chair of Physics** at the **Sorbonne University**. But he was **unwell**, and in a lot of **pain**. His fingers were **covered with sores** and his hands shook. Marie was **unwell** too – she **had lost a lot of weight** while isolating radium.

In **1903**, **Henri Becquerel** and **Pierre Curie** were nominated for the **Nobel Prize in Physics** – but not Marie. Pierre wrote to the committee to explain that it would be **ridiculous** not to honour Marie as well. In the end, the Nobel Prize was given to **all three scientists** for their work on **Becquerel rays**. This made Marie Curie the **first woman** to win a Nobel Prize.

THE NOBEL PRIZE FOR PHYSICS

1903

HENRI BECQUEREL

PIERRE CURIE

MARIE CURIE - FIRST WOMAN WINNER

Ra

X-RAYS

The prize money was a **huge help** to the Curies. They could afford to hire a lab assistant, and Marie was finally given a paid job at the university. They **didn't like being famous** though, they just wanted to get on with their work ...

19 April 1906

The worst has happened. My beloved Pierre has been taken from me.

This morning, as I dressed the girls for school, I kissed him goodbye as he left for the lab. I didn't know it would be the last time.

This afternoon a policeman knocked on the door to say Pierre had been hit by a horse-drawn wagon. I could not speak.

I do not feel able to face the future. How will I work without him? What will the girls do without a father? It is unimaginable.

I cannot forget, however, what Pierre has always told me, that even deprived, I ought to continue my work.

Marie was **devastated** at the loss of her husband, partner and best friend. But she wanted to keep herself **busy** and work was the best **distraction**. She went back to the lab the day after his funeral.

The **Sorbonne** offered her Pierre's job, making her the **first female professor** to work there. Marie took the job and set up a new lab in Pierre's memory, named the **Radium Institute**, to work on **radioactivity**. She continued making discoveries. She isolated pure radium metal in **1910**, and defined how to measure radioactivity. The measuring unit was named **the curie**.

But Marie was **unhappy**. A lot of French people were unkind towards her because she was a foreigner, and she still suffered **prejudice** in the scientific community because she was a woman. She faced a lot of criticism. She had also become very unwell. It was a hard time.

In **1911**, Marie was awarded the **Nobel Prize in Chemistry** for her discovery of radium and polonium. She was the first person ever to be awarded two Nobel Prizes and is the only person ever to win for **two different sciences**.

Marie's Wartime Diary

The First World War broke out in **1914**, and life in France changed dramatically. As the Nazi forces moved in towards Paris, I took the country's **entire supply** of radium (one gram) to a bank in the South of France for safekeeping. Then, I returned to the capital to help in the war effort.

I persuaded the government to set up **radiology centres** where wounded soldiers could be X-rayed for treatment. I was made Director of the new Red Cross Radiology Service. By late October I had my first **mobile radiology unit** – a van fitted with X-ray equipment that could travel to wherever it was needed on the battlefields!

Just one small PROBLEM: I didn't know how to operate X-ray machinery – or even how to drive!

I taught myself everything I needed to know, then I trained my daughter Irène as my assistant. By autumn **we were ready** to make our first trip to a battlefield to help soldiers.

Eventually there would be a fleet of **twenty** radiology units - the soldiers called them "**petites Curies**" (little Curies).

"Petites Curies!"

During the war I trained lots of **women** to work as radiological assistants. I also carried out radiotherapy - a medical technique that used limited doses of radiation to destroy damaged tissue.

To help pay for the war effort, I even tried to have my two gold Nobel medals **melted down**. But the bank refused to take them!

After the war, Marie kept working in the **Radium Institute** and set up the **Marie Curie Memorial Foundation**, which became a major international force in cancer treatment.

Marie and Pierre's daughter Irène won a joint **Nobel Prize in Chemistry** with her husband in **1935**, making Marie and Irène the only mother and daughter to both win a Nobel Prize. Sadly, Marie did not live to see her collect her prize. She died in **1934** of a blood disorder called **anaemia**.

Radioactivity is **extremely dangerous** at high levels. It can cause cancer and anaemia. People didn't fully understand the risks until years after it was discovered. By the **1920s**, many people had realised that working with radium was dangerous. New laws were made to protect people at work. Marie and Pierre didn't take **proper precautions** while working with radium – they didn't know they had to!

Whoops!

Marie called her discovery **"my beautiful radium"**, carried tubes of it around in her pockets and even **slept** with it **next to her bed** because its glow made a good nightlight. She used unshielded equipment while doing hundreds of X-rays during the war, which exposed her to more radiation. Marie died of the effects of **radiation exposure** and Pierre's sickness was **almost certainly** caused by **radium** too.

Marie's papers and notebooks from the **1890s** are still so radioactive that they are considered too **dangerous** to handle now. Even her cookbook is radioactive!

Marie was **buried** next to Pierre. Over **sixty years later** they were reburied in the **Panthéon** – the French national mausoleum for its **greatest men**. Marie was the **first woman** to be given her own place there.

Marie is one of the most influential scientists ever to have lived – she radiated **determination**, **bravery** and **brilliance**.

DR ELIZABETH BLACKWELL

THE DOCTOR WHO SHOWED WOMEN ARE CAPABLE TOO.

Elizabeth Blackwell was born in Bristol, England, in **1821**. In those days, many people thought girls didn't need an education, but Elizabeth's parents, Samuel and Hannah, made sure all of their nine children had **proper schooling**. Elizabeth loved reading and spent all her pocket money on books.

The Blackwell family were **abolitionists**, who believed that **slavery was wrong**. Along with many people in England, the Blackwell children gave up eating sugar from the West Indies because it was produced from sugarcane grown by slaves on plantations.

When Elizabeth was **eleven**, the Blackwells moved to New York, USA. There, Samuel opened a sugar factory, which used sugarcane that wasn't produced by slaves. He also offered shelter to **runaway slaves**.

Sadly, Samuel died when Elizabeth was **seventeen**. It was before he'd got his sugar business up and running and he'd lost a lot of money. Without their father, Elizabeth and her older sisters had to find a way to make enough money to support their big family – and fast! So, they set up a **school** in their home. Soon the Blackwell family were back on their feet.

Then, Elizabeth got a job at a school in Kentucky – but she hated it and soon came home. After that, she wasn't sure what she wanted to do. Everything changed when her friend got sick.

THE
USA

KENTUCKY

To raise the money for **medical school**, Elizabeth worked as a teacher in North and South Carolina – states that still practised slavery. She didn't like living there. She wanted to teach enslaved children to read, but that was against the law because the slave owners thought education would help the slaves **fight for their freedom**. Elizabeth set up a Sunday school instead to teach the children religion, but she felt bad that she didn't do more.

But I can tell you STORIES.

Elizabeth spent her time **studying medical books** while she saved up. But she had a **big problem:** she didn't like dealing with bodies. She hated being ill herself, and she remembered a time at school when her teacher brought in a bull's **eyeball** for the class to examine.

EURGH!

As an adult, Elizabeth wanted to **face up to her fears.** So, she decided to dissect a cockroach. At first, she thought she couldn't do it, but she was **brave.** She found that dissection was easier than she'd feared and **very interesting.**

FASCINATING!

THE COCKROACH

Finally, she saved enough money to pay for medical school. But now she had a new problem: **they didn't accept women.** Elizabeth applied to **twenty-nine** medical schools, but none of them would allow her to study there. But **Elizabeth didn't give up.**

She applied to **Geneva Medical College** in New York State. The teachers there asked the students to vote on whether to admit her. The students said yes! They even wrote Elizabeth a letter saying that **education** should be open to **everyone.** She found out later that many of them had only agreed because they thought her application was a **joke,** but that didn't matter – **she was in!**

HOW SPLENDID! I'm in!

Dear Miss Blackwell, we would like to offer you a place. Sincerely etc.

MY TIME AT GENEVA COLLEGE (as the only FEMALE doctor)

Things weren't easy at first. Some teachers made me sit apart from the male students in lectures and tried to ban me from practical demonstrations! Male students didn't know what to think of me at first.

PRACTICAL DEMONSTRATIONS

HONESTLY!

NO WOMEN

GASP!

PLEASE! There are things a lady should NOT see!

Many of the people who lived in Geneva, especially women, were unfriendly because they didn't approve of what I was doing.

I'm trying to help!

Despite all this, I quickly became friends with my fellow students and impressed my teachers. In 1849, I graduated top of my class. Even so, Geneva College turned down my sister Emily and didn't accept another woman student for years.

GO ELIZABETH!

DR Blackwell

EYE

FOOT

HAND

EAR

Elizabeth wanted to be a surgeon.
(She'd come a long way from **dissecting cockroaches**!)

She got a job in a hospital in Paris, France.
Elizabeth enjoyed her work – she was learning new skills every day. But she found it **difficult to fit in**. She didn't speak the language, and lots of the other doctors still didn't recognise her degree.

Then, **disaster struck!** Elizabeth was blinded in one eye while treating a baby with an eye infection. Elizabeth was very upset – with **poor eyesight** she could never be a surgeon. She would have to find a new area of medicine to specialise in.

St BARTHOLOMEW'S WASH ROOM

Once Elizabeth had recovered from the infection, she was offered a job at **St Bartholomew's** Hospital in London, England. There, she made friends with a young woman called **Florence Nightingale**.

Both women wanted to encourage **more women** to work in medicine, and they both cared about hygiene. They understood that **dirty hands** spread disease and that a lot of sickness could be prevented if people lived in **cleaner conditions**.

Hospitals were filthy. Doctors didn't yet understand **germs** and infection and many of them didn't wash their hands between patients. A doctor would examine a DEAD BODY or a person with a HORRIBLE DISEASE, like **smallpox**, and then go straight on to touch another patient with their dirty hands. Surgeons would do an operation on one person, and then use the same knife on someone else without even cleaning it!

Elizabeth knew how easy it was for infection to spread in hospital. So, she made it **her mission** to tell other doctors and nurses about the importance of **hygiene**. She wanted to make sure hospitals were clean to prevent patients from getting more unwell. She worked on this for the rest of her life. Today, hospitals and doctors have very **strict rules on hygiene**.

55

Elizabeth went back to New York, but nobody would give her a job. She had to set up her own medical practice. Things were **difficult** for a long time. People gossiped about her and sent her nasty letters, and many male doctors wouldn't work with her.

Elizabeth loved her work, but she found it very **lonely** working in New York. Finally, she adopted an orphan, **Kitty**.

Kitty always called Elizabeth **"Doctor"**. One day Kitty was present during the visit of a friendly physician.

At first, Elizabeth's practice didn't have many patients. People were still unsure about trusting a woman doctor. But she kept busy by giving lectures on health and hygiene. Slowly the practice grew and grew!

Elizabeth opened a **dispensary** where poor women and children could get medicine. Then, she raised money to turn it into a hospital.

Later, Elizabeth was joined by two
more talented women doctors, her sister
Emily and a German lady called **Marie
Elizabeth Zakrzewska**.

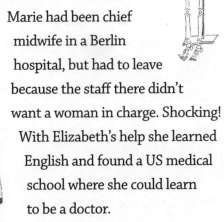

Marie had been chief
midwife in a Berlin
hospital, but had to leave
because the staff there didn't
want a woman in charge. Shocking!
With Elizabeth's help she learned
English and found a US medical
school where she could learn
to be a doctor.

It was Elizabeth's greatest hope that she
would inspire more women to become
doctors. So she went back to England
to do a special lecture tour. Elizabeth
became the first woman allowed to
work as a doctor in Britain.

Elizabeth wanted to open a **medical school for women,** but in 1861, the American Civil War broke out between the **Confederate** states, who wanted to keep slavery, and the Union states, who wanted to abolish it. Elizabeth put aside her plans and helped the Union. She **trained nurses** and worked to make the battlefield **hospitals cleaner** and save soldiers' lives.

The Union won, and slavery was legally ended in the USA in 1865. Once the war was over, Elizabeth set up her medical school for women. She was **Professor of Hygiene**. Her sister Emily taught obstetrics (medicine to do with pregnancy and childbirth) and diseases of women. It started with fifteen students and was a **great success**.

Elizabeth went back to England for good in **1869**, leaving Emily in charge of the hospital in New York. She became a doctor in London and set up a society to help people **live more healthily**. If people ate better food, kept clean and knew how to avoid catching diseases, they might not get sick in the first place!

Elizabeth became the Chair of **Gynaecology** at the **London School of Medicine for Women,** but had to retire after only a year because she became ill. She had an **active retirement,** writing books and getting involved in lots of campaigns. Kitty stayed with her all her life.

Elizabeth personally inspired over **470** women to become doctors in the UK alone, and showed the world that women could be just as good doctors as men. An **Elizabeth Blackwell Medal** is awarded to a woman doctor in the USA every year.

Very few people believed women could be doctors in Elizabeth's time. Even Elizabeth didn't think it was possible, **until she tried!**

Elizabeth Blackwell **changed the world** because she saw something was wrong and set out to put it RIGHT.

"It's not easy being a PIONEER... I would not trade a moment, even the WORST moment, for all the riches in the world."

Dr Blackwell

JANAKI AMMAL

THE BOTONIST WHO MADE THE WORLD A SWEETER PLACE

Janaki Ammal was born in Kerala, India, in **1897**, and was the tenth of thirteen children in the family.

Her father was very interested in **natural sciences**. He had a lot of books on the subject and made notes about how his garden plants grew. When Janaki was a child, many Indian girls didn't go to school. Janaki was lucky: she did get an education – her father was very pleased that she was interested in **botany** (the study of plants).

When Janaki was nineteen, she went to hear **Mahatma Gandhi** speak. He was the leader of the Indian Independence Movement, a group of people that wanted to **free** the country from British rule. Janaki was very **impressed** with what she heard. She decided she would follow Gandhi's example of **simple living** and **hard work** all her life.

SO INSPIRING!

Janaki went to college and completed **two degrees** in **botany**. After she graduated, she taught at the **Women's Christian College** in Madras (now Chennai).

Janaki, with TWO degrees.

But she wasn't there for long – she won an important **scholarship** that meant she could do a Master's degree in botany at the **University of Michigan**, USA.

There was just one problem – Janaki was supposed to be getting **married**! It was an arranged marriage to her cousin. If she refused, she might cause problems in her family. People would think she was **very strange** for putting her education before marriage and children. And many people in India didn't respect unmarried women.

But Janaki loved her work, and this was too good an **opportunity** to miss. She turned down the marriage and sailed to the USA to study in Michigan. An immigration official asked her if she was an **Indian princess** before he let her in to the country. SHE SAID YES!

I'm sorry. I can't MARRY you.

Oh.

Janaki got her Master's degree in **1925**. She focused her studies on the **chromosomes** of the shoo-fly plant.

A Master's was a **huge achievement** for an Indian woman at this time, but Janaki wanted to learn more. She went back to Michigan and started a **Ph.D**, the highest level of study, in botany and **cytogenetics**.

I'll explain properly what I researched later...

JANAKI'S STUDIES...

CYTOLOGY studies the structure and function of cells – how they are made, work, live and die.

GENETICS is the study of genes. It studies how living organisms, including people, inherit traits from their parents.

CYTOGENETICS is the branch of genetics where scientists study the genes inside cells and how they make the cells work.

When Janaki came back to India, she became Professor of Botany at the **Maharaja's College of Science**, Trivandrum. She stayed there for two years before taking up her next job – **working on sugar.**

Read about ROSALIND FRANKLIN on page 157 to find out more about GENES.

CYTOLOGY FOR BEGINNERS
HUMAN CELLS
PLANT CELLS
GENETICS
ADVANCED GENETICS
SCIENCE you NEED to Know
HOW Cells work VI
CYTOGENE

It was the **1930s**, and India was still part of the **British Empire**, but many Indians wanted their country to be independent. That meant they had to make India **self-sufficient** (producing things it needed instead of importing them).

India had grown **sugarcane** for 2,000 years, but the canes weren't as sweet as ones from other countries. India imported sugarcane from Java instead. However, that kind of sugarcane didn't grow well in India.

The **Sugarcane Breeding Station** was set up to develop a sweeter sugarcane that would grow well in India. Janaki went to work there in **1934**. Her knowledge on **chromosomes** was about to come in very handy ...

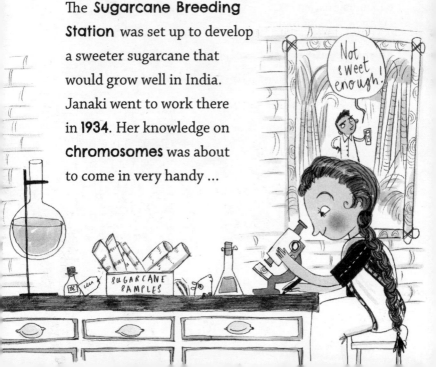

JANAKI EXPLAINS ...
CHROMOSOMES:

Every living thing is made up of cells. Each cell has a **nucleus**. The nucleus works like a brain – it controls everything that the cell does.

I told you I'd come back to this.

CELL NUCLEUS

Inside the nucleus are **pairs of chromosomes**. Each pair is made up of one chromosome from your mum and one from your dad.

If you unravel the chromosome, you find strands of a chemical called **DNA**. DNA carries all of the instructions that a living thing needs to grow, reproduce and function.

A **gene** is a short section of DNA. It contains a code that determines a certain **characteristic**, like eye colour or hair colour. There are thousands of genes in each chromosome.

Because living things get half of their chromosomes from each parent, they share some of their **parents' characteristics**. This is why you might have eyes like your mother, be tall like your father and have skin that looks like a mixture of both.

She has my straight hair.

She gets her LOVE of science from me.

MOTHER'S HAIR

FATHER'S EYES

Every living thing has a unique combination of genes. Even siblings have **different** genes (with the exception of identical twins). This is why you might have straight hair, while your sister has curly hair.

Some plants, like sugarcane, are different. Sugarcane's **chromosomes** don't come in pairs, they come in **bigger** sets. One sugarcane cell can have as many as ninety-two sets of chromosomes. This means that the plant has a very **complicated** mixture of genes.

Janaki's study of **sugarcane cells** helped people understand how sugarcane **chromosomes** worked. That meant she could work out which plant varieties to choose for **cross-breeding**.

Cross-breeding means getting two different varieties of plants or animals to **reproduce**. The idea is to **mix up the genes** and produce offspring with good qualities from both sides. The offspring is called a **hybrid**.

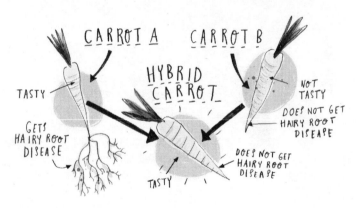

It's a WONDER HYBRID!

Janaki looked at many varieties of Indian sugarcane and developed hybrids that could **grow very well** in India and produce **sweeter** sugar. Her work **changed the taste of Indian sugar!**

Janaki was a **brilliant scientist** and she was starting to be **recognised for her work. The National Institute of Sciences of India** was founded in **1935**, and Janaki was chosen as a **research _fellow_** in the very first year.

JANAKI AMMAL RESEARCH FELLOW

A research fellow carries out GROUNDBREAKING research for a university.

But a lot of **men had problems** working with her. In India there were hardly any female scientists at this time. Many of her male colleagues said they didn't want to work with a woman as an equal, especially an unmarried woman. Janaki tried not to let their words bother her. **She just wanted to get on with her work.**

There were other problems too. India has a **caste system** where people are divided into different groups. That can mean some groups are considered more important and get the best jobs, while others are looked down on and are not given the same opportunities. Many Indian people think this is an **unfair** and **unjust** system and are trying to end it, but caste discrimination is a real problem.

Janaki belonged to the **Thiyya** community, who were based in **Kerala**. They were traditionally small farmers, or producers and sellers of palm wine. They were considered "untouchables" – people whose jobs were thought to make them dirty, so high-caste people refused to touch them.

Janaki's father had an important legal job and she'd had an **excellent education**. Even so, a lot of her colleagues still looked down on her. Some of them refused to work with her at all.

Janaki realised her **career** would never develop further at the **Sugarcane Breeding Station**, even though she had done so much **important work** there. **It was time to move on**.

Janaki was invited to speak at a conference in the United Kingdom in **1939**. She ended up staying there for **ten years**! She brought another Indian traveller with her when she came – a **palm squirrel** that she smuggled into Britain in the folds of her sari. She called it **Kapok**.

Janaki and Kapok lived in London during the **Second World War,** when German planes often bombed London at night. Janaki would hide under her bed during the bombings. The next day, she'd brush the broken glass off the shelves and get back to work.

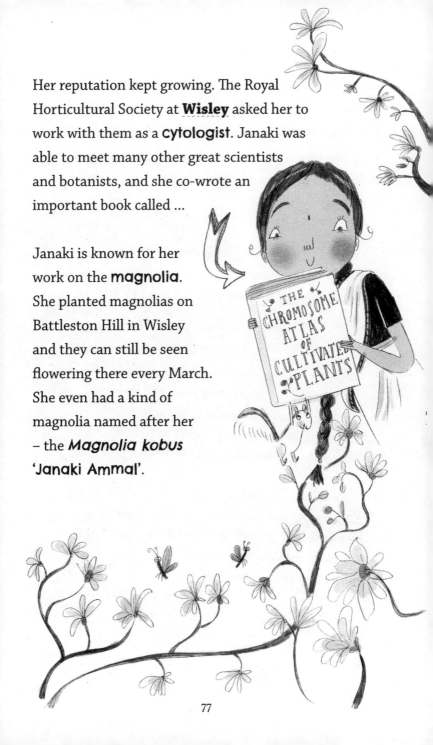

Her reputation kept growing. The Royal Horticultural Society at **Wisley** asked her to work with them as a **cytologist**. Janaki was able to meet many other great scientists and botanists, and she co-wrote an important book called ...

Janaki is known for her work on the **magnolia**. She planted magnolias on Battleston Hill in Wisley and they can still be seen flowering there every March. She even had a kind of magnolia named after her – the *Magnolia kobus* 'Janaki Ammal'.

THE CHROMOSOME ATLAS of CULTIVATED PLANTS

After ten years, Janaki wanted to return to India, which had become independent of Britain in **1947**. The new Prime Minister, **Jawaharlal Nehru**, asked her to come back and work on reorganising the **Botanical Survey of India**.

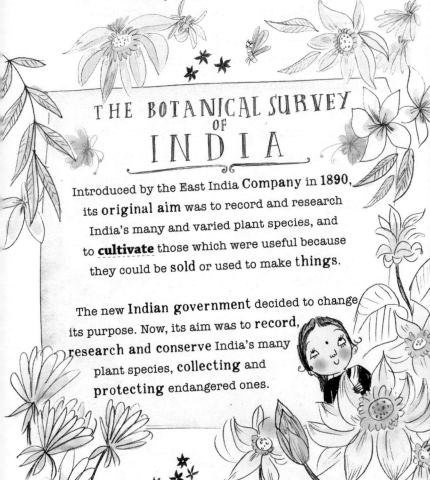

THE BOTANICAL SURVEY OF INDIA

Introduced by the East India Company in 1890, its original aim was to record and research India's many and varied plant species, and to **cultivate** those which were useful because they could be sold or used to make things.

The new Indian government decided to change its purpose. Now, its aim was to record, research and conserve India's many plant species, collecting and protecting endangered ones.

Janaki was awarded many honours in her career and died at the age of **eighty-seven** in a field lab at the **University of Madras**, working on her **beloved plants** till the end.

Janaki was an internationally respected scientist at a time when India struggled to accept women scientists. She was **fiercely independent** and **ambitious**, refused to accept that women should just get married and look after the home. Without Janaki's hard work, India's sugar wouldn't taste quite **so sweet** and we wouldn't know about many of the planet's most **beautiful** plants and flowers. She **blazed** a trail for **Indian science** and for **Indian women in science**.

KATIA KRAFFT

THE VOLCANOLOGIST WHO WASN'T AFRAID OF FIRE!

Katia Conrad was born in 1942, in Guebwiller, France. She was fourteen years old when she fell in love with **volcanoes**. She watched all the geological films she could find and got her parents to take her to Sicily, Italy, to see the famous volcanoes of **Etna** and **Stromboli**.

Maurice Krafft

Katia went to university in Strasbourg to study geology. There, she met another geology student, Maurice Krafft, who loved volcanoes as much as she did. Aged seven, Maurice had seen Mount Vesuvius near the Gulf of Naples, Italy, and had been hooked ever since. Maurice and Katia were soulmates.

As part of their studies, Katia and Maurice went to visit Stromboli. It is one of the most active volcanoes on Earth. It has been erupting almost non-stop since 1932!

WOW!

STROMBOLI

THE DANGERS OF VOLCANOES

Most people probably think active volcanoes aren't nice places to be.

They release sulphurous gas that smells of **rotten eggs**.

Volcanic gases are also **corrosive** and sometimes **dangerous**.

Of course, there's the **red-hot lava!**

There are **unexpected** jets of **super-hot** gases.

The ground can be **hard to walk on** because of ash and loose rock.

There can be pools of **boiling hot mud.**

83

But Katia and Maurice thought volcanos were fascinating, so they didn't mind getting really close to them. They collected samples of volcanic minerals and gases to take back for study.

When Katia graduated, she found it really difficult to get a job. In the late 1970s, there were only about 100 volcanologists in the whole world and only about twenty observatories. Katia and Maurice had to work for themselves.

They spent all their savings on another trip to Stromboli. They filmed the volcano's eruptions from close up and took some wonderful photographs.

Their photographs were printed in newspapers and magazines, and some were shown on television.

Katia and Maurice made enough money from their photographs and films to go on more trips. They also founded their own Centre for Volcanology in Alsace, France. They were volcano observers now, travelling the world to film volcanic eruptions.

They worked hard and were very busy, but they managed to find time to get married.

My LOVE for you will NEVER burn out.

WEDDING DAY

TECTONIC PLATES...

The surface of the **Earth** isn't one single piece of material, like the outside of a ball. It's more like a **jigsaw puzzle**, made up of lots of pieces that fit together. The pieces are called **tectonic plates**. These plates are always moving – in fact, they move at about one or two inches a year, all in different directions. Some **move apart** and some **bump together**.

The tectonic plates float on a layer of **magma**, which is rock that is so hot that it has melted and stays in liquid form.

When **tectonic plates** grate against each other, one plate typically pushes the other down. This causes **huge pressure to build up** in the **magma** and **gases** underneath.

Eventually, the pressure gets too much and the hot magma and gas **EXPLODES** through holes in the Earth's surface. This is how a volcano forms.

BOOM!

Volcanoes can also form in other ways. They might develop when **tectonic plates** pull apart from each other because this leaves weak points in the **Earth's crust** where magma can burst through. Sometimes they can occur in the middle of a **tectonic plate** that has particularly **hot magma** underneath.

TYPES of VOLCANO...

When the lava **cools** and **hardens** back into **solid rock**, this forms the mountains we call volcanoes.

Volcanoes have three states:

EXTINCT: An extinct volcano hasn't erupted since the last Ice Age (about 10,000 years ago) and is not expected to erupt again.

DORMANT (sleeping): A dormant volcano hasn't erupted in a long time, but geologists expect it will erupt again.

ACTIVE: An active volcano has erupted recently or is expected to erupt soon.

(Get ready to go!)

It is hard for volcanologists to **predict exactly** when an eruption will happen. <u>**Seismic activity**</u>, which describes tremors in the earth, goes on **all the time**. If a volcano hasn't erupted in living memory, people often don't see it as a **real danger**.

There are about **1,500** volcanoes that could be active in the world today. Between **fifty** and **sixty** volcanoes erupt every year. Often, the same volcanoes erupt **over and over** again.

Iceland has a lot of volcanic activity, but there hadn't been a proper eruption on the island of Heimaey for centuries – until January 1973, when the earth ripped apart. Katia and Maurice couldn't wait to get there!

A large crack in the Earth opened, just over half a mile away from the town of Heimaey. Lava fountains spurted in the air, some up to 150 m high.

Vast amounts of ash and cinders (called tephra) sprayed out of the crack and formed a cone 100 m high in just two days, covering the surrounding area in ash. Some good news – the people of Heimaey were all **evacuated**.

The film Katia and Maurice took of the lava fountains exploding behind the town, and the thick gritty tephra burying the houses was ASTONISHING!

The tephra fell so fast that Katia and Maurice had to crawl out of the first-floor window to get out as the door was blocked because the ash had mounted so high!

The new volcano was named **Eldfell (Fire Mountain)**. Its huge lava flows poured into the harbour. Heimaey was the Icelandic fishing fleet's most **important port**. If the lava blocked the harbour entrance, it would **destroy** the island's economy and damage the future of the whole country!

The Icelanders fought back! Thousands of tons of water were sprayed on the wall of lava. The front cooled into rock, forming a dam that stopped the lava behind it from rushing through. **The harbour was saved!**

Eldfell made headlines around the world, and Katia and Maurice's amazing pictures and film were a big part of that. The experience taught them a lot about how people can react to volcanoes, and they used it in their future work. When Eldfell had started erupting, the Icelandic government evacuated the island in just six hours, and only one person died.

Katia and Maurice travelled the world to document volcanic eruptions. They were often the first volcanologists to arrive at a new eruption, and always the ones who went closest to the lava flows. Some of the film they took is hard to believe.

In one particularly famous film, Katia is shown standing with a huge fountain of red-hot molten rock splashing behind her.

Katia was never afraid. For her and Maurice, the danger was worth it if it meant making

new discoveries.

Cool as a CUCUMBER →

"For me the DANGER is not important. I am AFRAID when I go in a car. But on volcanoes I FORGET everything."

Katia and Maurice once stayed inside the active volcano crater of Nyiragongo in the Democratic Republic of the Congo. All in a day's work for volcanologists!

The volcano contained a pool of molten lava that was hidden under platforms of solid rock. They pitched tents on one of the platforms. The walls of the crater reached **150** m above them, while the lava raged just **9** m below, its red heat reflecting off the walls ...

Tum te tum...

The level of the lava rose and fell unpredictably.

IT WAS THRILLING!

In 1985, the Nevado del Ruiz volcano in Colombia erupted. Over 23,000 people were killed. Volcanologists had warned the government in advance, but they hadn't listened. The problem was that the scientists could not say exactly when the volcano would erupt, and the people in charge didn't want to evacuate everybody in case it didn't.

Katia and Maurice filmed the terrible aftermath of the eruption. They knew about the destructive power of volcanoes, but this was the first time they had seen it cause such devastation to people.

After that, helping people who lived near volcanoes became an important part of their work.

We MUST help people!

In 1991, Katia and Maurice heard that there was a lot of seismic activity around Mount Pinatubo in the Philippines.

Katia and Maurice set out to persuade the President of the Philippines, Corazon Aquino, that she had to order an evacuation. They showed her their films of the TERRIBLE TRAGEDY around Nevado del Ruiz. Shocked, Aquino gave the order.

Not long afterwards, Mount Pinatubo erupted in the second largest volcanic eruption of the twentieth century. Tragically, 850 people died, but 60,000 people were evacuated in time. Many lives had been saved because Katia and Maurice helped get the government to listen.

Katia and Maurice's films were extremely important to help the public understand volcanoes and the DANGERS of living near active ones.

As well as making films, they did a lot of scientific work. Katia took samples of volcanic gases and minerals, measurements and readings. She documented how volcanic eruptions affected the environment by creating acid rain or ash clouds and pumping sulphur into the air.

Taking measurements sounds straightforward, but volcanic gases can be deadly. Animals are often killed by clouds of invisible, poisonous gas.

And taking rock samples isn't so easy if you're only a few feet from bubbling lava!

TOXIC GAS

HOT!

2 000°C!

Not all volcanoes are full of lava. Sometimes a crater bottom becomes coated with clay, making it waterproof. Rainwater slowly fills it up, forming a **crater lake**. In extinct volcanoes, these can become beauty spots. But if volcanic gases are still rising from the bottom, the lake can be a **DEATH TRAP**.

Kawah Ijen in Indonesia is a **volcanic lake**. It contains millions of tons of minerals as well as **hydrochloric acid** and **sulphuric acid**. Nothing can live in the lake and if you waded into it, it would **eat into your skin**.

As always, Katia and Maurice weren't afraid ...

DANGER!

Lake inside KAWAH IJEN

They wanted to take samples of the poisonous lake and so they took a rubber boat out into the middle of the steaming, stinking water ...

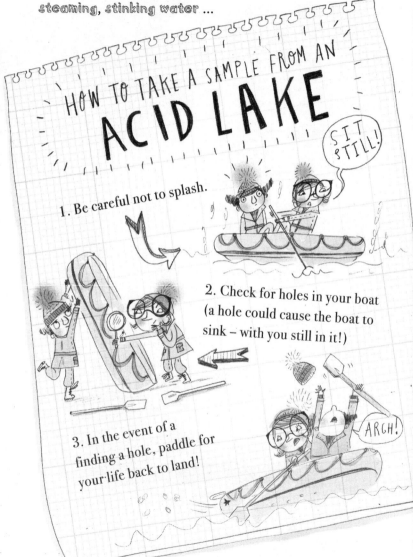

Katia and Maurice carefully lowered bottles on cords into the water, getting samples of the lake water at different depths. The experiment ended early when Katia discovered they'd lost one of the bottles – the acid had eaten through the cord.

It was a very dangerous thing to do, but the Kraffts saw it as an ADVENTURE. Maurice's greatest wish was to ride down a lava stream in a boat.

THE DAILY NEWS

TRAIL-BLAZING SCIENTISTS KILLED IN BLAZING ERUPTION

On 3 June 1991, there was an enormous eruption at Mount Unzen volcano in Japan. A huge tumbling flow of lava, gases, rock and ash with a temperature of 1,000°C poured down the side of the crater at more than 70 miles an hour.

Katia and Maurice Krafft, who were observing the eruption from a nearby platform, were killed instantly, along with forty-one other scientists, firefighters and journalists.

Over her twenty-year career, Katia witnessed forces of nature that most people wouldn't dare to get close to. Her **INCREDIBLE** films, photographs and research shocked, educated and protected people all around the world. Katia knew the risks of volcanoes better than anyone. She and Maurice chose to do what they did anyway because they **LOVED IT**. They died as they lived – bravely together, watching the volcano ...

Caroline Herschel

THE CINDERELLA WHO SWEPT THE SKY...

Caroline Herschel was one of the great scientists of her time, but when she was a child her mother didn't even want her to learn to **read**.

Caroline was born in Hanover, which is now part of Germany, in **1750**, and she was the eighth of ten children. Her father was an army musician and her mother ran the household. In those days, lots of people didn't think girls needed much education, but her mother didn't want Caroline to learn anything at all – not even dancing. She wanted Caroline to be the family servant and she was worried that if Caroline learned other skills, she would be able to leave home.

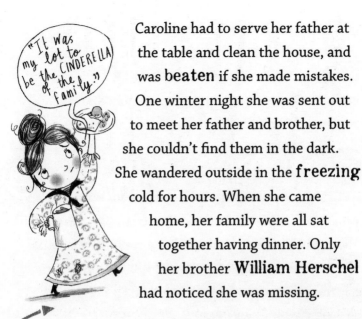

"It was my lot to be the CINDERELLA of the family."

Caroline had to serve her father at the table and clean the house, and was **beaten** if she made mistakes. One winter night she was sent out to meet her father and brother, but she couldn't find them in the dark. She wandered outside in the **freezing** cold for hours. When she came home, her family were all sat together having dinner. Only her brother **William Herschel** had noticed she was missing.

When Caroline was three years old she caught smallpox, which left her face badly marked. Then, when she was eleven, she caught <u>**typhus**</u> – the illness meant she never grew taller than **four foot** and **three inches**.

That's as tall as an average EIGHT year old child!

FOUR FOOT, THREE INCHES

In **1757**, Caroline's older brother William moved to Bath, England. He was a talented musician and composer. When Caroline was **twenty-two**, William asked her to come and join him. She had a good voice and he thought that she could be trained as a **soprano** singer.

At first her mother refused to let her go. Who would look after the house if Caroline wasn't there? The family couldn't afford to pay a servant – **Caroline worked for nothing!** Eventually, William offered to pay for a servant to replace Caroline. Her mother agreed. **Caroline was free.**

It wasn't an easy change. Caroline had never travelled before and could only speak a few words of English.

Caroline was lonely in Bath. She worked hard and didn't have time to make any friends. William gave her daily music lessons, as well as teaching her English and arithmetic. She also learned how to keep his accounts and spent hours writing out copies of his music. She had escaped her mother, but she was still expected to work for her family.

Other than in her lessons, **William Herschel** didn't spend much time with Caroline. He worked very hard organising concerts, and he had a new hobby – **ASTRONOMY**, the study of stars and planets.

William needed a **telescope** to examine the skies, but they had to be hand-made and were **EXTREMELY EXPENSIVE**.

Telescopes were difficult to make because they needed lenses that had to be ground out of glass. It was hard to get good enough lenses to see far-away objects.

A scientist called **Sir Isaac Newton** invented a kind of telescope that used mirrors. These were made of a **metal alloy** called speculum, which tarnished quickly and needed polishing all the time. And they had to be perfect because even tiny flaws in the mirrors would make the images blurry.

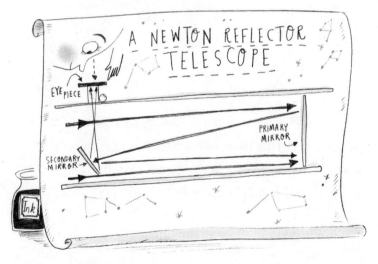

A NEWTON REFLECTOR TELESCOPE

EYEPIECE

SECONDARY MIRROR →

PRIMARY MIRROR

Ink

At first, William rented a telescope from a shop, but then he decided to build his own. He took lessons in making and grinding lenses and polishing mirrors. And, of course, he got Caroline to help. She even **fed** him!

Their house was soon taken over by astronomy. Some of their other brothers came over to England to help make these **complex machines**. Caroline learned to grind and polish lenses too.

Meanwhile, Caroline had built up a reputation as a singer and was **offered work** as a soloist by other musicians. She had a chance to become a **STAR**, but she turned it down – she only wanted to sing if William was the conductor.

But William didn't care about music any more. **He was only interested in astronomy.**

In **March 1781**, he noticed something in the sky. William thought it was a **comet**, so he wrote about it to other astronomers.

Soon they realised it was a planet beyond the orbit of **Saturn**. William had discovered a new planet in our solar system! It was later named URANUS. William wasn't the first person to see Uranus, but he was the first person to realise it was a planet and not a star.

William was elected a Fellow of the **Royal Society** and appointed the **King's Astronomer** with a salary of £200 a year. He gave up music and dedicated himself to astronomy.

It was the end of Caroline's **singing career** because she didn't feel brave enough to carry on without him. Singing had been her only way of earning her own money. Instead, she had to work as William's assistant. **She was very unhappy.**

She **ground** and **polished** mirrors and lenses.

She copied out **star catalogues**.

She worked out the **difficult calculations** astronomy needed.

She **fetched** and **carried**.

And she wrote down **William's observations** as he worked!

In **August 1782**, William made a small telescope called a Newtonian sweeper for Caroline and told her to sweep for comets. Sweeping meant sitting through the night to observe and record tiny changes in the pattern of the **starry** sky. Night after night, Caroline would sit watching and waiting ...

Caroline was still learning about the stars, so sweeping was **slow, tiring** work. She had to look up whatever she saw and she was constantly **interrupted** by William's demands.

Caroline was fed up. But as the year wore on her interest in the stars grew. She understood the work and she started to **look forward** to spending the **frosty nights** outside, watching the sky.

CAROLINE'S DIARY

A NEBULA

A NEBULA is a cloud of dust and gas in space. In the 18th Century the word nebula was used to describe any ASTRONOMICAL object that looked like a cloud instead of a single point. So GALAXIES outside the MILKY WAY were called NEBULA too.

1 August 1786 – An exciting evening below the stars! I counted 100 nebulæ AND saw an object which I believe will prove tomorrow night to be a COMET! Whooooosh!

A comet is a BIG ball of ice and rock travelling through space. When it comes near the Sun, it warms up and starts spitting out dust and gas, which creates a tail.

RAIN!

2 August 1786, 3 p.m. – Today I calculated 150 nebulæ but I fear it will not be clear tonight. It has been raining throughout the whole day, but seems now to have cleared up a little ...

3 August 1786, 1 p.m. – My soggy feet were worth it! The object of last night is A COMET.

A COMET

moving across the sky!

WOW!

It was a **triumph** for Caroline. She was the first woman ever to discover a comet and it made her famous. They called it, "THE FIRST LADY'S COMET".

In 1787, **King George** decided to pay Caroline a salary of £50 per year for her work with William, which made her the FIRST PROFESSIONAL FEMALE ASTRONOMER and the first ever woman in Britain to be paid a salary for scientific work. Finally, she had money of her own. She was thirty-seven years old.

Life changed a lot for Caroline after that. As well as making observations and doing calculations, William and Caroline were building a **40-foot telescope**! It was a huge construction that required vast amounts of work. It took nearly five years to build and the King paid an incredible **£4,000** towards the cost.

Suddenly, their house was **swarming** with labourers, workmen, blacksmiths and carpenters. There were always at least twenty-four men polishing the telescope, day and night. William never left the telescope – he even ate his food standing up because he didn't have time to sit at a table.

A FORTY FOOT TELESCOPE!

Caroline loved her work – she called it **"minding the Heavens"** – and she had quickly become a star among astronomers. She discovered **eight comets**! Finding a new comet was an exciting event. William was invited to Windsor Castle to point one of them out to the Royal Family. He called it, "MY SISTER'S COMET".

"My sister's comet!"

IT TWINKLES!

Other astronomers sent Caroline letters to say how much they **respected** her. They treated Caroline as an equal …

You advance scientific thought with so much success.

Everyone must ADMIRE you and your brother's knowledge.

SIR JOSEPH BANKS PRESIDENT OF THE ROYAL SOCIETY

ALEXANDER AUBERT ASTRONOMER

"Give me leave, noble and worthy priestess of the new heavens, to lay at your feet my small offering of eclipses of the sun…"

PROFESSOR SEYFFER

They are too kind.

With new stars being discovered all the time, astronomers needed an accurate list to work from. The first Astronomer Royal, **John Flamsteed**, had created a star catalogue, but it was in two parts and had **a lot of mistakes**. The catalogue desperately needed a proper index and corrections. That meant a lot of painstaking, boring work. William asked Caroline to do it while he carried on with the more interesting work of observations.

It took her nearly two years, but in **1798**, Caroline gave the Royal Society the index, plus a list of the mistakes and an extra **560 stars** the catalogue hadn't included.

The Herschels worked together until William died in **1822**. Caroline was devastated. She left England and returned to Hanover. There, she kept working to complete William's *Catalogue of Nebulæ and Clusters of Stars*, together with his son John.

In **1828**, she was presented with the **Gold Medal of the Royal Astronomical Society** for her discoveries and achievements. The Society said that nobody had ever done as much **hard, important work** for astronomy as Caroline had.

CAROLINE
HERSCHEL
a very IMPORTANT
ASTRONOMER

But Caroline was shocked to receive the medal and worried she **wasn't worthy** of it. Caroline grew up in a time when women were told they were less important than men.

Although Caroline never really learned to believe in herself, many other people recognised her GENIUS. Caroline was named one of the first female Honorary Members of the Society along with astronomer **Mary Somerville**.

Many years later, when women were demanding the right to vote and telling the world they were just as good as men, they named Caroline Herschel as one of the **fantastically great** women scientists who proved it.

TU YOUYOU

THE CHEMIST WHO SAVED MILLIONS OF LIVES

TU YOUYOU★ grew up in extraordinary times. She was born in **1930**, and by **1931** China was at war with Japan and with itself, as the **Chinese Communist Party** was trying to overthrow the government. There was a lot of fighting and many people suffered terribly and were hungry. Luckily, Tu Youyou didn't live in a badly affected area and her parents made sure she had a good education.

★CHINESE NAMES put the surname first, then the personal name – so Tu Youyou would be called Dr Tu, just like Jane Smith would be Dr Smith. Now, Tu Youyou is very old and a very important and educated woman. In Chinese culture it is a sign of respect to call her by her full name.

When Tu Youyou was sixteen she caught **tuberculosis**. She had to take two years off school to recover. But it was her long illness that inspired her to study MEDICAL RESEARCH.

If I could learn and have medical skills I could not only keep myself HEALTHY but also CURE many other patients.

After high school, she went to PEKING University Medical School to study pharmacy, the science of preparing and dispensing drugs. Her main area of study was pharmacognosy (you say it as *farmer-COG-no-see*). This is the study of drugs that are made from plants or other natural sources.

Tu Youyou was taught how to identify and classify medicinal plants. She also learned how to extract **ACTIVE INGREDIENTS** from plants and to study their chemical structures. The active ingredient is the part that has a chemical effect. Finding it is how we turn plants and herbs into medicines.

Most of Tu Youyou's courses showed her how to study and test the plants according to Western science. But China has its own **TRADITION** of medicine too ...

Traditional Chinese medicine (TCM) dates back thousands of years and is based on a set of beliefs, rather than evidence-based science. It uses herbal medicine, and mind and body practices to treat patients.

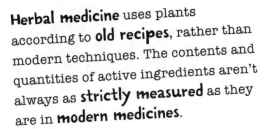

Herbal medicine uses plants according to **old recipes**, rather than modern techniques. The contents and quantities of active ingredients aren't always as **strictly measured** as they are in **modern medicines**.

There have been lots of different traditions and practices in **TCM**. Some of them were not scientific at all, like **demonology** (believing that **demons** caused illness). Others, like massage or special diets, are proven to help people.

NESE MEDICINE

Acupuncture:
Acupuncture uses metal needles to press points on the body. This is said to work with the **flow of energy** (called **qi**) in the body, and many people believe it helps **relieve pain**.

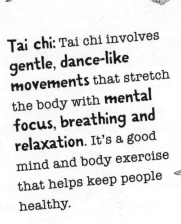

Tai chi: Tai chi involves **gentle, dance-like movements** that stretch the body with **mental focus, breathing and relaxation**. It's a good mind and body exercise that helps keep people healthy.

GRADUATION DAY

Tu Youyou graduated from university in **1955**. At this time, the Communist Party, led by **CHAIRMAN MAO ZEDONG**, had taken over China. After years of war, the country was very poor.

The population was over **500 MILLION** and there wasn't enough money to establish a modern healthcare system like the one China has today. There were not enough fully trained doctors or nurses, and the surgeries and hospitals were often poorly stocked.

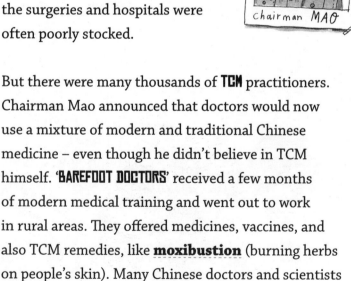
Chairman MAO

But there were many thousands of **TCM** practitioners. Chairman Mao announced that doctors would now use a mixture of modern and traditional Chinese medicine – even though he didn't believe in TCM himself. '**BAREFOOT DOCTORS**' received a few months of modern medical training and went out to work in rural areas. They offered medicines, vaccines, and also TCM remedies, like **moxibustion** (burning herbs on people's skin). Many Chinese doctors and scientists were upset.

They thought healthcare should be based on **TESTS** and **EVIDENCE** and that all doctors should complete proper medical training. But it was very **DANGEROUS** to disagree with the Communist Party. A lot of people were sent to prison for **SPEAKING UP** against the government.

The government set up a new **ACADEMY OF TRADITIONAL CHINESE MEDICINE** that brought together lots of ancient Chinese writings and ideas. Tu Youyou was sent to work there. She learned traditional Chinese medical theory and practice. She also got married to an engineer, **LI TINGZHAO**, and had two daughters. But while her life went on, the country was in **CHAOS**.

Tu Youyou's family

THE CULTURAL REVOLUTION

Chairman Mao's government wanted to show the world that Communism was a **SUCCESS**. But a lot of its policies were based on ideas that Mao **wanted to be true, not on facts**.

At the time, China's economy was mostly based on agriculture, but Mao wanted the country to move into **MODERN INDUSTRY**. The government **took land away** from farmers, and sent their workers to **factories** and **steel mills**. This meant that there **weren't enough** people growing and harvesting food.

We all had to wear matching suits.

People were also ordered to **kill sparrows** because they ate grain. But sparrows eat insects too. Without them, there was a **plague of locusts**.

As a result of these actions, there was a **terrible famine** and more than **30 million** people **starved to death**.

There is no food!

Help us!

I am SO HUNGRY

Lots of **BAD THINGS** were happening because of Mao's policies. Other politicians tried to change the way China was run. So, Mao started a new movement, called the **Cultural Revolution**. He said that Chinese Communism was being betrayed and that everyone who wasn't a good communist was the **ENEMY**. People were encouraged to **ACCUSE** each other so they weren't seen as traitors.

Intellectuals were particular targets because they were more likely to speak out against Mao's ideas. They were often **ARRESTED** and sent to do **HARD WORK** in the countryside. Schools and universities were closed. Libraries, religious buildings and many historical sites were **DESTROYED**.

It was a **DREADFUL PERIOD** where nobody was safe.
Nobody knows how many people were killed, but
historians think it was between **1 AND 10 MILLION**.
Many doctors and scientists were victims of the
Cultural Revolution, including Tu Youyou's husband,
Li Tingzhao. He was **SENT AWAY** from his family to work
as a labourer. Tu Youyou had to be very **CAREFUL** of
what she said and did so that the same thing
didn't happen to her.

But Tu Youyou was about to be faced with another big
problem that was spreading through China – **MALARIA**.

MALARIA

Malaria is a very serious disease caused by a parasite called **Plasmodium**, which is carried by **mosquitoes**. The mosquito picks up the Plasmodium by biting someone who already has malaria. When it flies off and bites someone else, it **passes on** the disease.

Mosquitoes are called a 'disease vector' because they spread MALARIA but don't cause it.

Not all mosquitoes carry malaria.

When the Plasmodium parasite gets into a person's **blood** it makes them very sick. They might experience symptoms such as a **headache**, **pain in their joints**, **chills**, **a fever** and even **sickness** and **diarrhoea**. If the person doesn't get medicine quickly they could suffer organ failure, brain swelling or breathing problems, which can be **fatal**.

Millions of people catch malaria every year (most of them in poor or developing countries) and, unfortunately, hundreds of thousands of them die.

Scientists had been looking for malaria treatments for years. **Quinine**, a drug made from the bark of a tree, was effective. However, it had **nasty side effects** and there was a shortage after the Second World War.

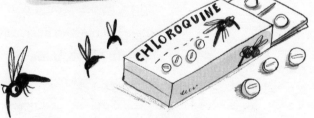

A drug called **chloroquine** was invented in the 1930s, but by the 1950s the Plasmodium were becoming **resistant** to it. The resistant Plasmodium reproduced and spread, which meant chloroquine medicine **didn't work anymore**.

We need new drugs!

Between **1954** and **1975**, North and South Vietnam were at war. The United States of America supported South Vietnam and China supported North Vietnam, which was also Communist. Many North Vietnamese soldiers were **DYING OF MALARIA** and their government asked China for help. Chinese officials set up a secret research project called **PROJECT 523** to find a new malaria remedy by experimenting with different TCM.

Tu Youyou was chosen to **BUILD** and **LEAD** a **PROJECT 523** research group. She was thirty-nine years old and didn't have a doctorate or postgraduate degree.

Normally she would not have been given such an **IMPORTANT** job, but a lot of the more experienced researchers had been caught up in the Cultural Revolution.

PROJECT 523

PROJECT LEADER: TU YOUYOU

CLASSIFIED TOP SECRET

Tu Youyou realised how **IMPORTANT** it was to find a
malaria cure when she spent six months on Hainan,
a tropical island off China's southern coast.

The work **BROKE UP** Tu Youyou's family even more.
Her parents cared for her one-year-old daughter,
while her four-year-old daughter was sent to a Beijing
nursery and lived with her teacher. Tu Youyou
didn't see her children for years.

Tu Youyou began her research by reading TCM literature and folk recipes, and interviewing practitioners. She made a list of over **2,000 HERBAL**, animal and mineral remedies for malaria. Then she started to **EXPERIMENT**.

For two years, Tu Youyou and her team tested hundreds of herbs. They found one herb, called **QINGHAO**, which had some effect in stopping the Plasmodium malaria parasites from reproducing. But the results varied a lot and it often didn't work.

The name Qinghao is used for six different species of the **ARTEMISIA PLANT**. The old recipes didn't identify which species they meant or say what part of the plant to use. Tu Youyou's team finally discovered that the active ingredient is only found in the leaves of one kind of **ARTEMISIA** (called sweet wormwood in English) – and only before the plant flowers.

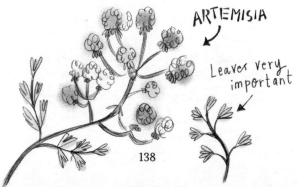

ARTEMISIA

Leaves very important

138

But even when they knew where the active ingredient was found, it still didn't work consistently. Tu Youyou went back to the **ANCIENT TEXTS**, searching for clues. She reread the *HANDBOOK OF PRESCRIPTIONS FOR EMERGENCIES* by the Chinese writer **GE HONG** from **340 AD**, which said that qinghao relieved malaria symptoms. One section jumped out at her …

"A handful of QINGHAO immersed in two litres of water. Wring out the juice and drink it all."

Most **TCM** preparation methods involve boiling herbs in water – but this one was steeped (**SOAKED IN LIQUID**). Tu Youyou had been using heat to make **QINGHAO** extract.

She experimented with '**COLD EXTRACTION**', making hundreds of different preparations of qinghao without boiling. Then, she tested her samples on rats. She tested **A LOT** of samples! Finally, **SAMPLE NUMBER 191** stopped Plasmodium from reproducing.

The next step was to make lots of qinghao extract
for testing. This was **VERY DIFFICULT** because so
many universities and labs were closed during the
Cultural Revolution. Without proper equipment, the
researchers suffered long-term exposure to harmful
substances, which was very **DANGEROUS**. Tu Youyou
and some of her team started to show unhealthy
symptoms. Still, they carried on **WORKING**.

There was another problem. Qinghao had been tested on animals, but it wasn't clear if it was **SAFE FOR PEOPLE**. If the team spent too long on testing, the malaria season would end and the study would be delayed by another year and **THOUSANDS** more people would die. Tu Youyou and two of her colleagues **VOLUNTEERED** to take the extracts themselves.

This was a very **BRAVE** thing to do. It could have made them extremely ill. But Tu Youyou and her team did what they felt they **HAD** to do.

Be careful Tu Youyou!

A week passed and **NO ONE WAS SICK**, so five more of the team took larger doses. Still, they didn't get sick.

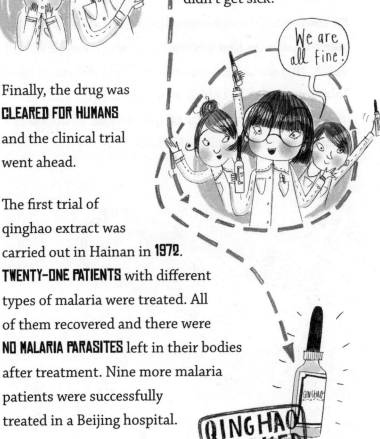

We are all fine!

Finally, the drug was **CLEARED FOR HUMANS** and the clinical trial went ahead.

The first trial of qinghao extract was carried out in Hainan in **1972**. **TWENTY-ONE PATIENTS** with different types of malaria were treated. All of them recovered and there were **NO MALARIA PARASITES** left in their bodies after treatment. Nine more malaria patients were successfully treated in a Beijing hospital.

QINGHAO WORKED

Tu Youyou and her team **ISOLATED** the active ingredient, named **artemisinin**. They went on to create a much more effective form of the drug so people could take lower doses.

In the West, Tu Youyou would have become **FAMOUS** right away. But under Mao's reign China was a very **SECRETIVE PLACE.** This was a military project – nobody was allowed to talk about it, and publication in scientific journals was **FORBIDDEN** in the Cultural Revolution. Tu Youyou's amazing malaria cure was **KEPT QUIET**.

TOP SECRET

FILE 523
(DON'T TELL ANYONE BUT THIS CONTAINS A CURE FOR MALARIA.)

144

Chairman Mao died in **1976**, and the Cultural Revolution came to an end. Tu Youyou's husband Li Tingzhao came home. Her family was **BACK TOGETHER** at last.

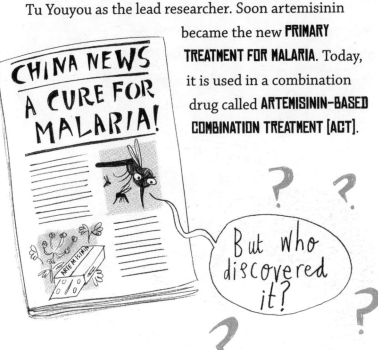

At last!

In **1978**, a Chinese newspaper published an official report about artemisinin and the first international report was published in **1982**, but it **DIDN'T NAME** Tu Youyou as the lead researcher. Soon artemisinin became the new **PRIMARY TREATMENT FOR MALARIA**. Today, it is used in a combination drug called **ARTEMISININ-BASED COMBINATION TREATMENT [ACT]**.

CHINA NEWS
A CURE FOR MALARIA!

ARTEMISININ

But who discovered it?

Tu Youyou was **PROMOTED TO RESEARCHER** (the equivalent of a professor) but she wasn't treated as a hero – she just went back to work.

Many years later, two American scientists discovered how important Tu Youyou's work had been. She was awarded the **NOBEL PRIZE IN PHYSIOLOGY OR MEDICINE** in **2015**. Tu Youyou was the first Chinese winner for research done in China and the first Chinese woman ever to take the prize. Tu Youyou was **SHOCKED** to receive the award.

But artemisinin was discovered thanks to her **INSPIRED IDEAS** and her **DEDICATION** leading the team. Tu Youyou is one of the greatest lifesavers the world has ever known.

ROSALIND FRANKLIN

Rosalind Franklin was born to a Jewish family and grew up in London, England, in the **1920s**. Her parents taught her and her four siblings to always form and argue their own opinions. Rosalind learned to **speak up** for herself.

"Rosalind is ALARMINGLY CLEVER. She spends all her time doing arithmetic for pleasure, and invariably gets her sums right."

Erm, but she's only six!

147

Rosalind at school

Rosalind was **excellent** at science, languages and sport.

CHEMISTRY
SCIENCE
NEWNHAM COLLEGE

She did very well at school and won a **scholarship** to Newnham College, University of Cambridge, to study chemistry.

My EARS!

La LALA!

Music lessons

But there was one subject that she was **TERRIBLE** at ... music! Her music teacher was the famous composer **Gustav Holst**. Rosalind's singing was **so bad** that he once asked her mother if she had tonsillitis or hearing problems.

At the time, **Adolf Hitler** was the leader of the Nazi political party, who were in power in Germany. Under his regime, Jewish people and other minorities were being **persecuted**. The Franklins took in two child refugees, and Rosalind gave her university scholarship to a **Jewish refugee student**.

When the Second World War began, many Jewish refugees came to Cambridge. One of them was **Adrienne Weill**, a French scientist who had studied under **Marie Curie.** She and Rosalind became friends.

In **1941**, Rosalind sat her final exams and got a second-class degree. She was very **disappointed** not to get a First. Rosalind had spent so long making each answer **perfect** that she'd run out of time and didn't finish all the questions. Even so, she got the **top result** in the university in Physical Chemistry and she was given a research fellowship.

The fellowship was a great opportunity, but Rosalind didn't like the job and decided to do **war work** instead. She researched coal and also worked as an **air raid warden**.

COAL CRISIS!

YOUR COUNTRY NEEDS YOU (AND COAL)

Coal is incredibly important!
It is the main source of **energy** for heating homes and powering factories, and is needed to run trains and power ships.

Britain, we have a problem.
Many coal miners have joined the army and now there **aren't enough** miners to dig the coal out. From now on, no coal miners may join the army. Some people who sign up for the army will be sent to coal mines instead.

Once the war was over, Rosalind went back to study and received her doctorate. Then, she got a job as a researcher in Paris. She used **X-ray diffraction** to study the structure of coal and how to turn it into an important material called **crystalline graphite**.

DIFFRACTION

FIG 1: A SLIT

LIGHT

SLIT

Light bends when it passes around an edge or through a slit. This bending is called **diffraction**.

Rosalind used diffraction to look at **molecules**. When she aimed X-rays at a crystal, it diffracted the X-ray in many directions. Each type of crystal **diffracted X-rays differently**.

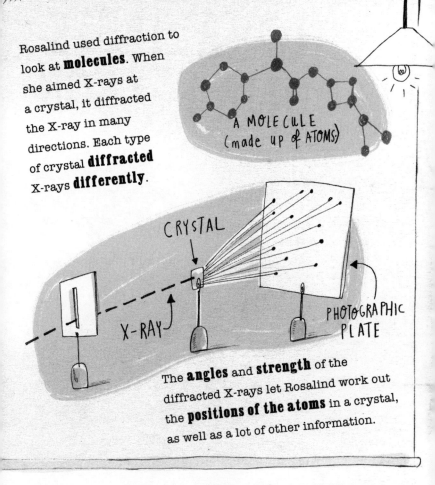

A MOLECULE (made up of ATOMS)

CRYSTAL

X-RAY

PHOTOGRAPHIC PLATE

The **angles** and **strength** of the diffracted X-rays let Rosalind work out the **positions of the atoms** in a crystal, as well as a lot of other information.

Rosalind was very happy in Paris and made many friends in her new job. After three years, she was offered a three-year fellowship at **King's College London** to work on proteins. She decided to come home. But when she arrived, the boss of the section asked her to change jobs. He wanted her to investigate **DNA** instead.

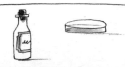

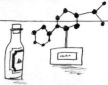

ROSALIND'S DNA LESSON

DNA is short for **deoxyribonucleic acid**. To understand why it's important, we need to know about **cells**.

A CELL

Some cells help us see and others help us hear. Some **build muscles**, or help us **digest food** or **make our skin**. There are over **200 cell** types in the body.

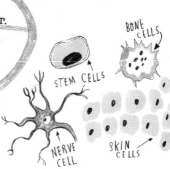

BONE CELLS

STEM CELLS

NERVE CELL

SKIN CELLS

We are all made from lots of cells. About **30 trillion**, or **30,000,000,000,000**.

MUSCLE CELLS

BLOOD CELLS

AMAZING

But how does each cell know what to do?

That's where **DNA** comes in. Each cell contains DNA to give the cell its **instructions**. It's a bit like the code that tells a computer what to do.

DNA CELL

GENES

Strings of DNA make up genes. Each cell in the human body contains about **25,000** to **35,000** genes, and each gene has a **job to do**.

The DNA in a gene gives instructions for making **proteins** in the cell. **Proteins are the building blocks** for everything in your body – eyes, teeth, hair, skin and muscle. Those proteins help our bodies **grow, work and stay healthy**.

By the **1940s**, scientists knew that **genes controlled our cells** and that DNA was somehow responsible, but they didn't know how it worked. The **STRUCTURE OF DNA** held the secret of life. And a lot of scientists wanted to understand it.

SCIENTISTS hadn't yet proved DNA looked like this.

How will we figure this out?

We MUST work out the structure of DNA.

At the time, the Assistant Lab Chief at **King's College** was a man called **Maurice Wilkins**. He had been examining DNA samples using **X-ray diffraction.** When he learned how good Rosalind was at that, he told the boss that he wanted Rosalind to join his **DNA team**.

But when the boss offered Rosalind the job, he told her that she would **take over the DNA work**. When she arrived, Rosalind assumed she would be running the DNA team, but Maurice thought he would – and that she would report to him. **IT WAS A DISASTER!** Rosalind felt Maurice was trying to order her about. Maurice didn't understand why Rosalind was so difficult when she was meant to work for him!

They should have talked about it. But Maurice **hated arguments** and ran away from them instead of dealing with problems. Rosalind **liked arguing**. She could be very blunt, which meant she sometimes hurt people's feelings. **The pair couldn't get on**. Soon their research assistant **Raymond Gosling** had to carry messages between them. It was an **awful atmosphere** to work in. Rosalind used to cry when she got home.

157

THE SECRET STRUCTURE OF DNA...

Several researchers thought that DNA had a **helix** (spiral) structure in some way.

Just like computer code, DNA has its own **special language**. But its alphabet has only four letters – **A**, **C**, **T** and **G**.

A and **T** are always in pairs and **C** and **G** are always in pairs.

But DNA isn't a **straight ladder**. By January **1953**, Rosalind was pretty sure that DNA was **curved in a complicated spiral**, which we call a double helix.

I think DNA is a DOUBLE HELIX.

Rosalind and Raymond took a **photograph of DNA** that clearly showed its double helix structure. It was called '**Photograph 51**'.

PHOTOGRAPH 51

"The MOST BEAUTIFUL X-ray photograph of any substance ever taken."

Rosalind thought a lot more work needed to be done to **make sure** her findings were correct, but she'd already decided to leave **King's College**. This meant handing over her DNA work to Maurice and **starting again** on something else. It was worth it to **get away** from the horrible environment.

Other scientists were working on DNA too. Back in **1951**, Rosalind had given a lecture about DNA in Cambridge. A pair of DNA researchers called James Watson and Francis Crick built a model of DNA using some of her ideas. However, Watson hadn't made notes from her lecture, so they got some of the details **wrong.** Their model had a **triple helix.**

Watson and Crick invited Rosalind and Maurice to see the model. Rosalind **wasn't impressed**, so she turned down their offer to work together.

INTERESTING!

Not really.

In January **1953**, Watson found out that an American scientist called **Linus Pauling** was going to publish a paper on DNA. He went to King's College to ask Rosalind and Maurice to **work with him and Crick** so they could publish the answer first. But Rosalind still **didn't want to work with them**. She thought Watson was rude and disrespectful and said, **"No thanks."** However, while Watson was at King's College, Maurice showed him Photograph 51.

Meanwhile, Francis Crick got hold of **Rosalind's unpublished** research, which was full of data that let him make the calculations he needed. The report and the photo weren't secret, but Watson and Crick **didn't ask Rosalind for permission** to use them.

Thanks to Photograph 51 and Rosalind's data, Watson and Crick were **sure that DNA had a double helix structure**.

Watson and Crick built a double helix model. When Rosalind and Maurice saw it, they immediately agreed it was **right**.

In April **1953**, Watson and Crick published their paper describing the double helix model of DNA. They mentioned Rosalind and Maurice's work in a **footnote**, but they didn't say **how important** it had been. Rosalind and Maurice published their data on DNA in the same issue of the journal. There was a party at King's College to celebrate the three articles. Rosalind had left by then. **She didn't go**.

163

Rosalind's new job was at **Birkbeck College**, London, working in a pair of converted old houses that didn't make very good labs. Once someone left a tap on upstairs and **flooded** her lab!

But she was much **happier**. She started working on the **structure of viruses** and made several important discoveries along with a scientist called **Aaron Klug**, who became one of her best friends.

In **1956**, Rosalind learned she had **cancer**. She hadn't used a protective lead apron while doing X-rays at King's College and some people think the **radiation** made her sick, just like **Marie Curie**.

Rosalind was incredibly **brave** during her illness. When she could no longer walk, she **crawled** up the stairs between labs. Her research group published several important papers in the last two years of her life. She died in April **1958**, aged only **thirty-seven**.

SCIENTISTS WHO DISCOVERED... THE STRUCTURE OF DNA...

CRICK

In **1962**, James Watson, Francis Crick and Maurice Wilkins were awarded the Nobel Prize in Physiology or Medicine for discovering the structure of DNA. The rules of the **Nobel Prize** say that only people who are alive can be nominated, so **Rosalind wasn't included**. Watson and Crick became extremely famous, while Rosalind's work on **DNA** was forgotten.

A few years later, Aaron Klug found a draft paper of hers that showed how much Rosalind had contributed to the DNA discovery. He published it and Rosalind's work was finally given the **credit it deserved** – including by Watson and Crick.

Watson agreed she should have been one of the Nobel Prizewinners. He donated a DNA sculpture to the **University of Cambridge**, with an inscription saying that Rosalind and Maurice's work was a **crucial part** of the discovery.

WHY WASN'T I THE FIRST TO THE DISCOVERY?

I was a **perfectionist**. Watson and Crick didn't mind guessing and making mistakes. They really wanted to be the **first ones** to discover the secret. I thought it was more important to make sure every step was **exactly right**.

Watson and Crick worked as part of a **team**, discussing ideas. I struggled to work with Maurice. Most of the time we didn't speak at all and when we did, **we argued**. This made it harder for us to find the answer.

I was **miserable** at King's College. It's hard to have great ideas when you're sad.

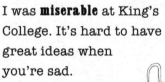

In **1982**, Aaron Klug won the **Nobel Prize in Chemistry** for the work he'd started doing with Rosalind, based on her ideas. If she had lived, they would probably have **shared** the Nobel Prize and it might have been her second one.

It took a long time for Rosalind's work on DNA to be given credit, but she is now one of the **most famous female scientists in the world**. She has statues and medals and awards and buildings named after her, plus a boat, an asteroid and a Mars Rover. She died young, but she'd already helped discover the **secret of life**. Just imagine what she could have done if she'd had more time ...

Other FANTASTIC GREAT

DOROTHY VAUGHAN

SALLY RIDE

KATHERINE JOHNSON

PIERRE CURIE

MARY JACKSON

ALLY
PEOPLE...
FLORENCE NIGHTINGALE
JOHN FLAMSTEED
MARY SOMERVILLE
SIR ISAAC NEWTON
ADRIENNE WEILL
AARON KLUG

Glossary

Abolitionists: people who wanted to end slavery.

Anaemia: a blood disorder caused by a deficiency in red blood cells or haemoglobin in the blood. It causes people to feel extremely tired and weak.

Artemisinin: a drug that cures malaria.

Astronomy: the study of objects outside Earth, like stars, planets and comets.

Atom: a tiny particle and the basic building blocks of the universe. Atoms are made up of even tinier particles called protons, neutrons and electrons.

Botany: the study of plant life.

British Empire: the old name for for all the regions in the world once ruled by Britain.

Cancer: a disease where cells in the body grow too quickly and can destroy healthy cells.

Caste system: social structuring practised in India, where people are categorised into different groups. Their position in society is decided based on their family background.

Chinese Communist Party: the founding and ruling political party of the People's Republic of China.

Chromosomes: molecules made of DNA that carry the information cells need to grow and reproduce.

Civil Rights Movement: a protest movement that aimed to end racial segregation and discrimination against black Americans in the 1950s and 1960s.

Comet: a small object in space, usually made of dust and ice, that travels around the Sun.

Compound: a substance formed when two or more elements are chemically bonded together.

Cross-breeding: scientific breeding programme that enables two different varieties of plants or animals to reproduce.

Cultivate: to grow, develop and improve crops.

Cultural Revolution: a political movement that took place in China between 1966 and 1977. It was designed by Chairman Mao as a way to maintain Communism in the country.

Cytogenetics: the branch of genetics where scientists study the genes inside cells and how they make the cells work.

Cytology: the study of how cells are made and how they work.

Diffraction: the bending of light waves when they pass around an edge or through a narrow gap.

Dispensary: a place where medicines are prepared and given out.

DNA: the short term for deoxyribonucleic acid. It is found in every cell, in every living thing, and carries genetic information.

Doctorate: the highest academic research degree that is offered by universities.

Element: a substance made from a single type of atom. An element can either be a gas (such as oxygen), a solid (such as iron) or a liquid (such as mercury).

Emit: to give out or produce something, such as a gas.

Evacuate: to empty something or somewhere. When we make people leave a dangerous place, that is an evacuation.

Famine: a very serious food shortage.

Fellow: a member of a learned society, college or university.

Gravity: the force of attraction between objects. The Earth is very big so it exerts a strong force of gravity, pulling people and things towards it.

Hybrid: the offspring of two different types of plants or animals.

Intellectuals: highly educated people, usually experts or scholars in a particular subject.

Magma: the molten rock under the Earth's crust.

Master's degree: an advanced degree given by a university for specialist work.

Metal alloy: a kind of combined metal made by mixing other metals together. Bronze is an alloy of tin and copper.

Mineral: a solid substance, such as rock, that comes from nature but is inorganic (not created by plants or animals). Gold, diamonds, sulphur and salt are all minerals.

Moxibustion: a form of traditional Chinese medicine that involves burning dried herbs on a person's skin.

NASA: the space agency based in the USA.

Nebula: It comes from the Latin word for smoke. In the 18th century, the word nebula was used for any astronomical object that looked like a cloud instead of a single point – so galaxies outside the Milky Way were called nebulæ too.

Ore: a kind of rock containing a large amount of a particular mineral.

Peace Corps: a volunteer programme run by the US government where Americans go to help out in other countries.

Peking: the old name for the capital city of the People's Republic of China, currently known as Beijing.

Prejudice: judgement made against a person without knowing them. It is prejudiced when people treat others badly or look down on them because of things such as their race, religion, gender, body shape, or other things they can't help.

Qi: the concept of a vital life-force that flows through the body, which is central to traditional Chinese medicine.

Radioactive: when a material sends out highly dangerous rays of energy (radiation).

Ray: a beam of energy.

Royal Society: the oldest national scientific society in the world. Its full name is the Royal Society of London for Improving Natural Knowledge.

Satellite: an object, like a moon, comet or man-made space vehicle, that orbits a larger body, such as a planet.

Saturn: the sixth furthest planet from the Sun in our solar system.

Segregation: when one group of people are kept apart from the rest. Until the mid-20th century, schools in the USA were segregated so that black children went to different schools from white children.

Seismic activity: Earth tremors or earthquakes.

Smallpox: a contagious skin disease that covered people with blisters and often killed them. Smallpox has now been largely eradicated.

Soprano: someone who sings the highest notes in a piece of music, usually a woman.

Space Race: the twentieth-century struggle between the Soviet Union and the USA that aimed to be the first to send people into space, land people on the moon, and launch the most satellites.

Tectonic plates: the huge plates of solid rock that form the Earth's crust.

Telescope: an instrument to help people see things that are far away.

Tuberculosis: a life-threatening disease that mainly affects the lungs.

Typhus: an infectious disease that causes extremely high fevers, and is often deadly.

Uranium: a radioactive element.

Weightlessness: the feeling of being without weight, when someone, or something, isn't affected by gravity.

Wisley: the headquarters of the Royal Horticultural Society, based in Britain.

X-ray: a form of radiation that can penetrate objects light can't. X-rays can be used to take pictures of the insides of things, like suitcases or bodies, without opening them up.

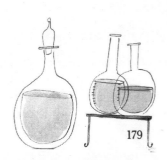

Further reading

If you want to find out more about any of the fantastically great women in this book, the books and websites below are brilliant resources.

Books

Frost, Adam. (2018), *The Awesome Book of Space*. London: Bloomsbury.

Greenberg, Imogen and Greenberg, Isabel. (2021), *Marie Curie and Her Daughters*. London: Bloomsbury.

Ignotofsky, Rachel. (2017), *Women in Science: 50 Fearless Pioneers Who Changed the World*. London: Wren & Rook.

Pankhurst, Kate. (2016), *Fantastically Great Women Who Changed the World*. London: Bloomsbury.

Pankhurst, Kate. (2018), *Fantastically Great Women Who Made History*. London: Bloomsbury.

Pankhurst, Kate. (2019), *Fantastically Great Women Who Worked Wonders*. London: Bloomsbury.

Sanchez Vegara, Maria Isabel. (2017), *Little People, BIG DREAMS: Marie Curie*. London: Frances Lincoln Children's Books.

Websites

National Geographic Kids. https://www.natgeokids.com/uk/category/discover/science/

BBC Bitesize. https://www.bbc.co.uk/bitesize/subjects/z2pfb9q

Britannica Kids. https://kids.britannica.com/kids/

NASA Kids' Club. https://www.nasa.gov/kidsclub/index.html

Dr Mae. http://www.drmae.com/

European Space Agency Kids. https://www.esa.int/kids/en/home

The Marie Curie Foundation. https://www.mariecurie.org.uk/

The Royal Horticultural Society. https://www.rhs.org.uk/

Thank you

I'm delighted that you are holding the first
Fantastically Great Women chapter book in your hands
right now. Over the past few years I've got to know
the Fantastically Great Women as I've researched and
illustrated their lives for the picture books that sparked
the idea for this book. Having more pages in this new
format to introduce the amazing female scientists and
their incredible achievements has been a real treat.
None of this would have been possible without the
team of fantastically great people behind this series ...

Firstly I'd like to thank the amazing Bloomsbury
Children's Non-Fiction team who have looked after
me and the Fantastically Great Women series so far
with great affection and care. Isobel Doster and Katie
Knutton (this book's editor extraordinaire and design
genius), Sharon Hutton and Saskia Gwinn, you are all
Fantastically Great Women!

There is SO much fascinating content in this book, I've learned so much as we've put it together so a MASSIVE thank you to Kate Paice for her incredible research and writing skills. I am in total admiration of your ability to turn complex scientific theories into content we can all understand.

Huge thanks to the publicity and marketing teams at Bloomsbury for shouting very loudly about the Fantastically Great Women books and getting them noticed. Emily Marples, Jade Westwood, Grace Ball and the rest of the team thank you!

Without my incredibly hard working agents at Plum Pudding Illustration the Fantastically Great Women series of books wouldn't have happened at all, so a massive thank you to Hannah Whitty and Mark Mills, and the rest of the Plum team.

About the author

KATE PANKHURST is the bestselling author and illustrator of the trail-blazing and internationally successful **FANTASTICALLY GREAT WOMEN** books. The series has been nominated and shortlisted for whole host of awards, including: the British Book Award for Children's Illustrated and Non-fiction Book of the Year, the SLA Information Book Award and IBW Book Award.

Most days, Kate can be found writing in her studio in Leeds with her spotty dog, Olive. She loves a good story, the funnier the better, and gets her best ideas by doodling – because even quick, wonky drawings can spark amazing ideas.